YATHĀBHŪTAM

BRAHMAN AND CITTAMATRA
The Convergence of the Eastern Esoteric Traditions

Sho Fu

Copyright © 2012 by Robert J. La Sardo

All rights reserved.

No part of this book may be reproduced or transmitted in any form or by any means, electronic or mechanical, including photocopying, recording or by any information storage and retrieval system, without written permission from the author, except for the inclusion of brief quotations in review.

Published in the United States and the United Kingdom by WingSpan Press, Livermore, CA

The WingSpan name, logo and colophon are the trademarks of WingSpan Publishing.

ISBN 978-1-59594-460-3

First edition 2012

Printed in the United States of America

www.wingspanpress.com

Library of Congress Control Number: 2012931163

1 2 3 4 5 6 7 8 9 10

YATHĀBHŪTAM
truly, as it is

DEDICATION
*To those who can move past the immediate need
for survival effort and have the energy
to sit back and consider;
the one in a hundred-thousand.*

*When we search for fire with a lighted torch,
every place that we look is the wrong place.*

The power of desire is threefold at the time of retraction, for the sake of rest, when she rests on the right side of the Lord's Chest, in the shape of Srivatsa, She is the power of yoga.
– Sita Upanishad #35

"Those who believe in the birth of something that has never been in existence, and coming to exist, finally vanishes away – which leads them to assert that things come to exist, things pass away, according to causation— such people have no foothold in my teaching."

Lankavatara Sutra --Chapter 3, Verse 7

CONTENTS

PROLOGUE.. 1
INTRODUCTION.. 3
ALL AT ONCE.. 5
YATHĀBHŪTAM... 7
THE OTHER HEART SUTRA... 8
THE CITY OF THE GHANDARVAS.. 9
B.T.W.. 10
IR-RESPONSIBILITY.. 11
THE EIGHT VIJNANAS.. 12
ARYABHAVAVAVASTU.. 12
THE BLISS OF THE NATURAL CONDITION............................... 14
POPPING THE QUIFF (Q.W.F. : quantum wave function)*........... 17
RUPA/VIJNANA: The "Two" Skandhas; Cutting to the Chase...... 19
D.T. SUZUKI.. 20
LIVING PRACTICE... 25
FANDANCE.. 26
B.T.W. II... 27
BRAHMA/SHIVA... 31
MORE SPIRITUAL MATH.. 33
TEN.. 35
LANKA-YOGACARA... 37
ADVAITIC CHRISTIANITY.. 38
ADVAITIC CHRISTIANITY 2... 39
ADVAITIC CHRISTIANITY 3... 40
MORE INVERSIONS.. 41
THE CONDITIONAL... 42
THE UNCONDITIONAL.. 42
THE PIVOT... 43
ETERNAL UNTHINKABLE... 44
EX-SISTERE.. 45
THEATER... 46

350 PT. HALVETICA BOLD	47
SHEDDING LIGHT AND LOSING TIME	48
THE FREQUENCY/TIME AMBIGUITY	49
BISHOP BERKELEY	50
INTRODUCTION TO THE SUMMATIONS	52
THE MIND IS MOVING	53
ALL IS BRAHMAN/SELF	61
THE CORE OF THE LENG YEN CHING	62
DZOGCHEN	63
RUMOR	65
FINAL THOUGHTS	66

Prologue

At the center of unenlightenment is profound arrogance and complacent stupidity, the recoil of apparent embodiment. The most effective way to remove this crippling perspective for the twenty-first century mind is to use the power of our remarkable conceptual talents against itself analogous to a mental auto immune response with intentionality; a self-diagnostic that is truly directed to the foundation upon which our complacencies rest. Upon reflection, these are space, time, causation, identity, upward evolution and its religious counterpart; a self-existing entity that creates everything from outside itself and can be petitioned; all directed and conjured up by an entity inside each one of us.

    Remarkably, all of this is predicated on the imagination of a real independent objective world or reality, persisting as a conditioned response even after the advent of quantum mechanics.

    We can face a wall and meditate forever with no results with the possible exception of the magnification of our pettiness if we are tacitly convinced that there is a world out there and that we are meditating, which is striving for enlightenment from the foundation of unelightenment; as fruitless a venture as striving for happiness from unhappiness.

    The unnerving relentlessness of the Mahayana Buddhists and the masters of the other great traditions was because of this tendency to look at everything from unenlightenment and then try to get out of the box. Usually, all that was accomplished was to take the box with them. In short, everything that is comfortable and familiar; the lock on complacency, must be challenged.

YATHĀBHŪTAM

With deep investigation, space and time melt and causation is hilarious. Mass and energy do not come from any place that can be pointed to; the masquerade is over. This vast perplexity is all discarded and released by seeing into its impossibility by rigorous penetration; and this can be accomplished because everything is built upon opposition. In other words, it carries with it its own inevitable destruction, notwithstanding its convincing disguises. Neither; nor, is not an artifice, it is a reality.

Note: The foundation that was developed in *The Mind Seal* and *The Kings Question* is taken for granted in what follows, which is presented in an unstructured series of footnotes, essays and poems, long and short.

YATHĀBHŪTAM

Introduction

"The enlightenment attained by the Pratyekabuddhas, Buddhahood,
Arhatship, and the seeing of the Buddhas—
these are the secret seeds that grow in enlightenment, but
it is accomplished in a dream."

      #222 Sagathakam

YATHĀBHŪTAM

ALL AT ONCE

To see Yathābhūtam is to at once recognize all as Mind itself; the Solitary.

The only difference between a Buddha and an ordinary sentient being is that the former knows that he/she has never uttered a word.

When the realization is embraced, no proof is required; the bottom has fallen out, it cannot be any other way. Proof is for things.

Words, bound by discrimination, are the carrier of transmigration. As soon as something is imagined to be out there; ex-sistere, it must be powered in its seeming motion independent of the perceiver, and since it is imagined as external, its power must be inside the external; a more subtle external. This is ego or possession.

"The ignorant, like a corpse, are bad logicians." – Lanka p. 144

Emotion is inherent in the moment of creation; the mirror Consciousness; intelligent omnipresent infinity contemplating itself; that very separation, looking at itself as an object, simultaneously reflexes the longing for eventual return as a blueprint for a great process. This is the longing or lengthening.

Apparent separation from our source in all the frequency realms or Buddha lands.

Causes and Conditions:
Cause: False discrimination; exclusive world concept and then forms, appearance and objectivity.
Condition: nama-rupa
This is the field of imagination, causation, relativity; the parsing of the energy of Consciousness.

The Void is contemplating itself right now in the midst of this cluttered manufactured reality.

Non-ego in Buddhism is, paradoxically, to get away from nihilism and ultimately away from materialism. The ego, as imagined, is contained, and the container is transient; that is why the source is relegated to the Alayavijnana.

No self-nature: in a state of incessant becoming things cannot last to have self-nature.

When the perspective of Yathābhūtham is upheld, the samadhis swell and the feeling of being is uppermost because the Being/Energy is no longer reduced to spiritual enthropy; spent in the imagination.

For the wise, objects are not judged as they are in themselves; they are nothing but their cognition. If things are imagined to have their own self-nature, what is alone is not seen. Continued discrimination as a source of wisdom is an indication that what is alone is not seen. Formlessness is just the disappearance of discrimination.

The Mahayana is not a definite philosophical doctrine, but is only set in motion by the thoughts of sentient beings. This is why Buddha was the dreadful murderer of philosophy and the destroyer of the gods.

The *MANAS* is Mahayana Buddhism is the very gesture of self-contemplation, discrimination; the birth of the mirror consciousness and the time/frequency realms or parallel worlds. •

YATHĀBŪTHAM

The world does not arise from god, or spontaneously, or from time, or from a supreme spirit or any imagined causal agency…close…. CLOSER…sfah!
    Feeling and being the vastness, all is allowed; but it will always be right relationship. What do you want that isn't already yours? •

YATHĀBHŪTAM

THE OTHER HEART SUTRA

#274 (sagathakam) – There is no rising of the causation chain, nor are there any sense-organs; no dhatus, no skandas, no greed, no samskrita [things tied to the chain of causation].

#279   And there are no Buddhas, no truths, no fruition, no causal agents, no perversion, no nirvana, no passing away, no birth.

#278   And there are no twelve elements, and no duality either, of limit and no limit, because of the cessations of all the notions that are cherished by the philosophers I declare there is Mind only.

#279   The passions, path of karma, the body, creators, fruitions—they are like fata morgana and a dream; they are like the city of the Gandharvas.

#280   By maintaining the Mind-only, the idea of reality is removed; by establishing the Mind-only permanence and annihilation are seen in their proper relationship.

#281   There are no skandas in nirvana, nor is there an ego soul, nor any individual signs; by entering into the Mind-only, one escapes, from becoming attached to emancipation.

#282   It is error (dosha) that causes the world to be externally perceived as it is manifested to people; Mind is not born of the visible world; therefore, Mind is not visible.

These are not a list of negations; they are impossibilities. When we discuss what objects are or are not, we are discussing something that has never been established independently, as axiomatic. The observer is the raison d'etre for the appearance of the object; good Buddhism, good Quantum Mechanics. •

THE CITY OF THE GHANDARVAS

Watch how the long-ing |―――――――| is produced in the mirror consciousness and the avalanche of *vasana* that comes to its support.

Any qualified object; physical, psychic, is sustained by the qualifier; kept apart and maintained moment to moment. But the qualifier and qualified cancel when not maintained. •

"There is nothing grasped, nor grasping, nor one who grasps; there are no names, no objects; those who carry on their groundless discriminative way of thinking lack intelligence." – #263 – Sagathakam

B.T.W.

How can anything that has no independent nature be momentary? Discrimination is momentary.

There is a feeding frenzy on multiplicities of objects which are not there; ego soul and what belongs to it. Thus tainted; karma, greed, anger and folly; all by discrimination with names. But these are unobtainable owing to their mutual conditioning; they must be held apart to obtain. Their origin is not god, time, atoms, or supreme spirit, but discrimination. All of the above are placed outside; ex-sistere, and will be subject to non-finality. •

IR-RESPONSIBILITY

We are the supplier and measurer of all things and then relinquish authority. We cognize things and then go on to describe them as if we had nothing to do with them. The description of all of their properties are all our perceptions; time-slipped and place-locked.

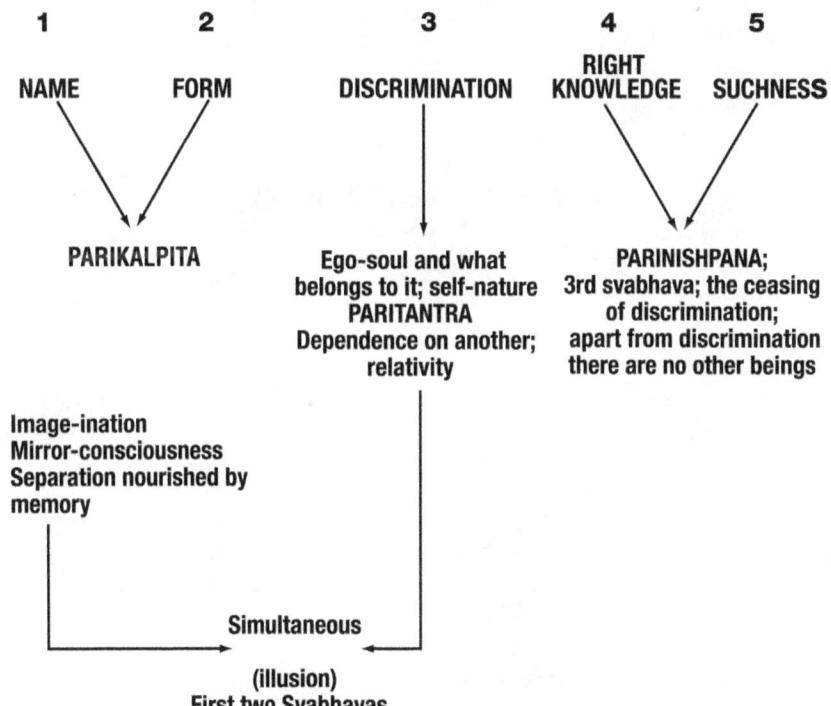

YATHĀBHŪTAM

THE EIGHT VIJNANAS

O TATHAGATAGARBA --- what transmigrates

1. MANAS
2. MANO-VIJNANA
3. EYE-VIJNANA
4. EAR-VIJNANA
5. NOSE-VIJNANA
6. TONGUE-VIJNANA
7. BODY (TOUCH)-VIJNANA

MOMENTARY:
False discrimination as cause;
objectivity as condition

HABIT ENERGY/MEMORY
existence, desire, form, theorizing

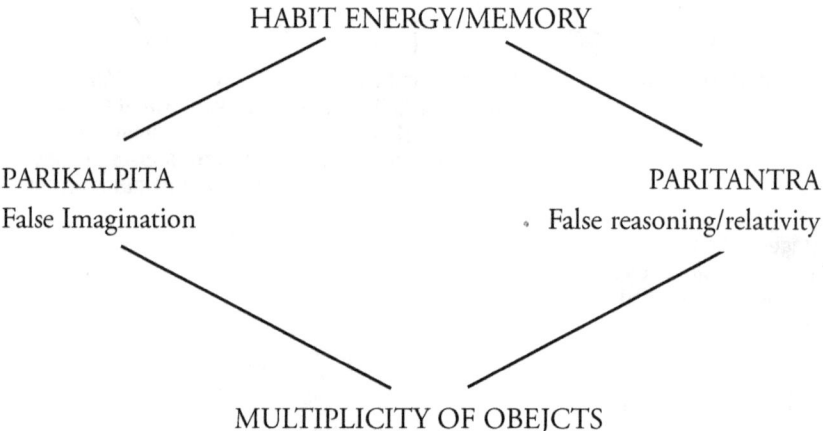

Idea of body-property-abode; that all objects exist, all at once, is an idea rising from habit energy.

    If all objects existed at once, there would be a cause outside Mind itself. Awareness cannot question itself, only an imaginary entity can question itself; the clowning bifurcation, until Awareness dissolves it. Without the entity there is no *world*.

ARYABHAVAVAVASTU

The world has its cause in the memory of what we separated; we are trying to measure something that we are casting; our shadows.

Everything that is subsequently taught is in response to this; causation, no causation.

The twelvefold chain of origination is taught in *response* to discrimination; grasped and grasping.

"Understanding comes in mid-sentence. Words are illusion; they're all cradles of rebirth." – Bodhidharma

This understanding is not dependent on a conclusion but the undermining of the questioner!

> Turning the wheel of the Dharma; or the curve
> of the Chaitanya Shakti

When the light is turned on; all the circuitry is in place; upper cranial triangle to the heart on the right side (sinoatrial node)*--then there is a rechanneled interference pattern permeating the vasanas where pure Bliss Awareness is prominent; a spiritual transformer.

The mirror is inherently bright and reflects everything but it only becomes a mirror when we look at it and all that is ever seen is ourselves.

---

* See *The Science of Soul*, by Shree Swami Vyas Dev Ji Maharaj; illustration No. 1

Ultimately, we are incapable of doing anything wrong because the person is a phantom; which means, paradoxically, that the only thing that we can do wrong is to continue to imagine our personhood which is neither right nor wrong; a barren women's child.

THE BLISS OF THE NATURAL CONDITION

Paravritti/Vichara

When attention is inverted and the question is asked while all conceptual answers are seen as clowning substitutions, the force current from the Heart, the house of Brahman, to the cranial triangle becomes intensified. In a most intense form the Ajna Chakra points north and the mouth opens.* (See illustration).

The Supreme Being is unmanifest as such to habitual discrimination but when the paravritti or the vichara is engaged regularly, the Aham Spurana is the first sign of its manifestation. But this manifestation is not apart; it is felt to boundless expansion where so-called objects of any kind are dissolved as fast as they arise, unobstructions that no longer have a hold, and become background rather than foreground in the disposition of ananda or Being/Bliss.

2

The turning around from objectivity where Awareness is free enough to see the house being built in each moment; lit up by the Atma Nadi is the beginning of the Paravritti where separation cannot be maintained and Awareness manifests its character; a bathing in innate bliss that is no longer concerned with desultory discrimination which was the substitute for the character of Being/Suchness. Here, Awareness turns concrete into glass.

"In the world of Brahman there is a lake whose waters are like nectar, and whosoever tastes thereof is straight away drunk with joy; and beside that lake is a tree which yields the juice of immortality" – Chandogya Upanishad

The Mind Seal

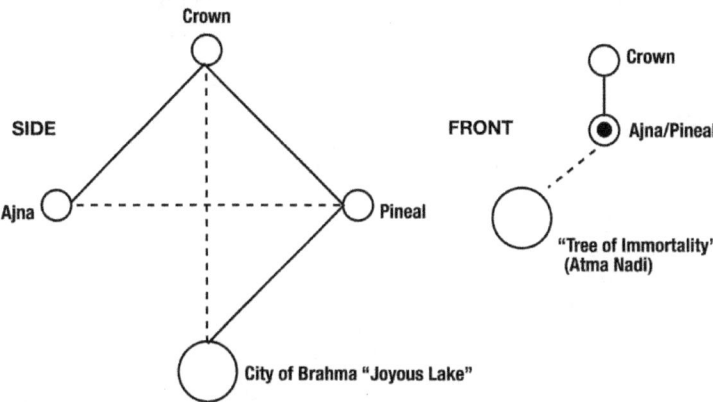

*Years ago I was shown a Tibetan statue showing this, but had no idea what it was until it appeared in my meditation.

3

Every remedial gesture is treating the symptoms of an imagined separation from Source; *"When the two make peace in this house"*. When the struggle with symptoms is finally undermined, the feeling of yourself from Source becomes the template which rejects the fall from this expansive Bliss of innate Being; the loss of its flavor in hardcore duality; a wrong relocation that does not feel right. If all of our relationships are embraced from here, it will be painfully realized what we have been relating to.

"When names and appearances are seen as unobtainable." – The Lanka

When the raison d'etre for something (nama-rupa) is locked into its own cognition, "it" can only be obtained as an idea or concept; that very name and appearance re-established. It moves in time and exists as long as the concept is re-established. Separation is a myth. Everything is built from that initial gesture of imagination; as soon as we take possession the world take place.

Every moment of arrested attention is resolved and done with, but the cloud of habit energy from beginningless time, or the gesture of recording, surrounds us like a spectre; its memory being a substitute for being present; thus a multiplicity of objects is suggested but not experienced. Experience can only be one-thing-at-a-time with memory as reference/matrix.

Things are only independent of us in retrospect. •

POPPING THE QUIFF (Q.W.F. : quantum wave function)*

Who's MINDING the store.
The fact that new things can be experienced on a recording of an event even if we were there during the recording might seem to indicate that this was an independent local event that we are subsequently witnessing. But in the 21st century non-locality in or out of quantum theory is much more than a suggestion. The violation of Bell's inequality is based on repeatable experiments and a sound mathematical foundation.

Remember, we are producing time and space locks. We created the concepts of the past and location; constructed the recording machine and then became aware of an event which is always reliving a memory whether we call it a current experience, a reverie or a recording. If we think that we missed something we have image-ined it; it was an image of an event that was assumed there without knowing it; the transcendence of knowledge, after the act of rehearing. Before the rehearing it was not an issue at all.

But, you still insist, it is there preserved on the machine and I say that this is an incomplete abstraction; the abstraction of non-participation; its interdependence taken out of context and made independent. The tape recorder or similar device is a better recording apparatus than our brain receiver because it is free of distractions. Nevertheless, this is not one recorder listening to another; this is non-temporal Awareness which as the *Grundlage* transcends both. Machines do not interact independent of the observer.

Notwithstanding the violation of Bell's inequality, how can Reality be local with its foundation being variables? Time, space and causality are contextual variables; *kein grundlage.* If there is no space, time or causality as such, there is no locality. Space and time as such was demolished by Einstein and local causality became a function of the observational operator that collapsed the wave function into a phenomenal reality in the double slit experiment.

It was said that J.S. Bell "invented a single argument based on experimental results that indirectly demonstrates the necessary existence of non-local connections" **…because noumenon cannot be seen as such.

YATHĀBHŪTAM

Phenomenon is the appearance of noumenon; local phenomenon built on non-local noumenon; but the local phenomenon is no less Reality than the non-local noumenon...the appearance of *MIND ITSELF.* •

*Term used by Dr. Fred Allen Wolff
**Nick Herbert

RUPA/VIJNANA: The "Two" Skandhas; Cutting to the Chase

#718; Sagathakam

"The Rupa-skandha (matter) and the Vijnana-skandha—there are these two Skandhas and not five; they are different names for the Skandhas; of this I have talked in a hundred ways"

#684; Sagathakam

"Not being born, suchness, reality, limit, and emptiness—these are other names for form (Rupa); one should not imagine it to mean a nothing..."
Or a something.

Antakarana

For every bad/good experience throughout our entire life, we had to create an entity to experience it. The experience either dissolves as a temporary bifurcated structure in the SELF, channeled into the unqualified root feeling or it is possessed and entified as your self, undigested.

All trouble is indigestion.

Compassion

The imaginary person who caused you the trouble has the same trouble. Compassion is only possible with the un-person; anything else is specific empathy that has the possibility of being shared but won't cross certain lines; where *you* live.

YATHĀBHŪTAM

D.T. SUZUKI

"The Alayavijnana is its own subject (cause) and object (support)" ... shadows of MIND—only; try chasing a shadow. Since you are creating it, it will always be the same distance from you.

●●●

The soul in the Skandhas is like the imagination of the abode of music being located in the horn. This abstraction is a misuse of the conceptual function in an attempt to objectify the Source. The esoteric Buddhists never said that there was no *SELF* but that it could be viewed as an object inside its own creation; the Skandhas.

The appearance of the *SELF* in the Upanishads; the house of Brahman and the idea of the Sphurana is an interface when separation is inseen and relaxed and not something inside or alongside of the Skandhas.

The type of analysis that seeks to avoid the objectification of the Source also indirectly negates it. The quality or taste of Self or Being or Mind itself becomes the subject of silence in the classical Madhyamika analysis.

The Confusion

To bring out this difficulty; the negation of the imagination of a place for Self in a non-objective world and the simultaneous revelation of its glory, we will quote some passages from the Upanishads, the sagathakam of the Lankavatara and the Sat-Darshana Bhashya; a difficulty as old as communication. Keep in mind that these are Buddhist and Vedantic sources.

What would conventional letter of the law Buddhism say to the following: *"Those who hold the theory of non-ego are injurers of the Buddhist doctrines, they are given up to dualistic views of being and non-being; they are to be ejected by the convocation of the Bhikshus and are never to be spoken to"*...yes!, it is the absence of non-ego!!

In his footnotes, Suzuki voiced concerns over this and similar passages as they stood.

"Trying to seek five ways for an ego soul in the accumulation of the skandhas, the unintelligent fail to see it, but the wise seeing it are liberated"...you see what you are not; the seeker is the sought.

"*When the Yogin reflects upon the MIND, he does not see the MIND in the mind; an insight comes forth from the perceived [The World]; whence is the arising of this perceived [World]...*" he realizes that the perceived cannot perceive!

The key to the seeming contradictions is in #746 of the Sagathakam. The oneness of two great traditions that were subsequently separated through confusion by the simple minded is also flatly stated: "*The ego (ATMA) characterized with purity is the state of self-realization; this is the Tathagata's womb (garbha) which does not belong to the realm of the theorizers*"...Atman and Tathagata-garba in one sentence!

And finally, "*As the womb is not visible to the woman herself who has it, so the ego soul is not visible within the Skandhas to those who have no wisdom*"...but those that have wisdom are what-they-are; with the paravritti, the Skandhas are arising in them.

In the Upanishadic tradition, the ontological realization came forth as immediate expression unhampered by the analysis of subsequent generations trying to remove the corruption that inevitably crept in when interpretation overpowered realization regardless of what the tradition was called. Atma purified is Brahman. HE is the Tathgata-Garba.

"*He is the principle of life. He is speech and he is mind. He is real. He is immortal. Attain him, o my friend, the one goal to be attained*". Here, the Paravritti is stated in positive terms after the insight of Mind-only; the door is open to be overpowered by a greater reality once the short circuit of identification is relaxed.

"*The self-luminous being who dwells within the lotus of the heart, surrounded by the senses and sense organs, and who is the light of the intellect, is that Self.*"

In the Vedanta, the antakarana is the temporary, generated structured that gets in the way of reintegration; in Buddhism it is Manas. Like the head of Brahama looking in both directions, it can either continue looking in the direction of self-possession (enclosed) or become SELF possessed (self-luminous being). It is the third head; facing us, that is the resolution of the bifurcated perspective, similar to the Tibetan double dorje; the resolution of duality at the center of the eternal unthinkable.

In the Svetasvatara Upanishad and in other Upanishads, there is a complete summation of Mind-only and the yoga interface that is the turning around (paravritti) toward the eternal face of Brahma.

"*I have known, beyond all darkness, that great Person of golden effulgence. Only by knowing him does one conquer death. There is no other way of escaping the wheel of birth, death and rebirth.*

There is nothing superior to him, nothing different from him, nothing subtler or greater than he. Alone he stands, changeless, self-luminous; he, the Great One, fills this universe. Though he fills the universe, he transcends it. He is untouched by its sorrow. He has no form. Those who know him become immortal. Others remain in the depths of misery. The Lord God, all pervading and omnipresent, dwells in the heart of all beings. Full of grace he ultimately gives liberation to all creatures by turning their faces toward himself…this Great Being, assuming a form the size of a thumb, forever dwells in the heart of all creatures as their innermost Self. He can be known directly by the purified mind through spiritual discrimination. Knowing him, men become immortal."

…and in the Brihadaranyaka Upanishad: "*The self-luminous being who dwells within the lotus of the heart, surrounded by the senses and sense organs, and who is the light of the intellect, is that Self. Becoming identified with the intellect, he moves to and fro, through birth and death, between this world and the next. Becoming identified with the intellect, the Self appears to be thinking, appears to be moving.*"

…and in the Katha Upanishad: "*Radiating from the lotus of the heart there are a hundred and one nerves. One of these ascends toward the thousand petaled lotus in the brain. If, when a man comes to die, his vital force passes upward and out through this nerve, he attains immortality; but if his vital force passes upward and out through another nerve, he goes to one or another plane of mortal existence and remains subject to birth and death. The Supreme Person, the size of a thumb, the innermost Self, dwells forever in the heart of all beings. As one draws the pith from a reed, so must the aspirant after truth, with great perseverance, separate the Self from the body. Know the Self to be pure and immortal—yea pure and immortal*".

…and in the Chandogya Upanishad: *The Self within the heart is like a boundary which divides the world from THAT. Day and night cross not that boundary, nor old age, nor death…in the world of Brahman there is a lake whose waters are like nectar and whoever tastes thereof is straightaway drunk with joy; and beside that lake there is a tree which yields the juice of immortality...*

This body is mortal, always gripped by death, but within it dwells the immortal Self. This Self, when associated in our consciousness with the body, is subject to pleasure and pain; and so long as this association continues, freedom from pleasure and pain can no man find. But as this association ceases, there cease also the pleasure and the pain."

With such an economy of expression it might be difficult to understand that a phrase like *"...nothing different from him"* is the summation of Citta-Matra; Nirvana is Samsara or 'The World is unreal, only Brahman is real, the world is Brahman." Coming from the *via positiva* the truth is declared; coming from the *via negativa*, it is suggested at the end of an elaborate process of elimination.

Through the words of the greatest Siddha/Sage of the 20th century, we can see the best of all the vision of all the great traditions coming together. The following is taken from the Sat-Darshana Bhashya and talks with Maharashi. These are the details of the Paravritti.

...But the body is matter (Jada), it never knows, it is always the known. (recall Huang Po; the perceived cannot perceive).

...But the moment the ego self tried to know itself, it changes its character; it begins to partake less and less of the Jada, in which it is absorbed, and more and more of the Consciousness of the Self, the Atman...you need have no doubt about it. The Real Self is there in the Heart behind the Jeeva or ego self.

In the spirit of the Maya like Samadhi of the Lanka...
...From the Heart, the Self-center, there is a subtle passage leading to the Sahasrara, the Shakti Sthana. The ordinary man lives in the brain unaware of himself in the Heart. The Jnana Siddha lives in the Heart. When he moves about and deals with men and things, he knows that what he sees is not separate from the one Supreme Reality, the Brahman which he realized in the Heart as his own Self, the Real. (just substitute Mind-only for Brahman and deepest seat of Consciousness for Heart).
...when you go deeper you lose yourself, as it were, in the abysmal depths, then the Reality which is the Atman that was behind you all the while takes hold of

you. It is an incessant flash of I-consciousness, you can be aware of it, feel it, hear it, sense it, so to say; this is what I call Aham sphoorti…You can feel yourself one with the One that exists; the whole body becomes a mere power, a force current; your life becomes a needle drawn to a huge mass of magnet and as you go deeper and deeper, you become a mere center and then not even that, for you become a mere consciousness, there are no thoughts or cares any longer—they were shattered at the threshold; it is an inundation; you, a mere straw, you are swallowed alive, but it is very delightful, for you become the very thing that swallows you; this is the union of Jeeva with Brahman, the loss of ego in the real Self, the destruction of falsehood, the attainment of Truth…this is the passage of liberation (Moksha). This is called Atmanadi, Brahmanadi, or Amrita Nadi. This is the Nadi that is referred to in the Upanishads.

The process described above is the dissolution of the imaginary center; Manas or Antakarana that *places* the Source inside or outside of anything; the doer is unable to move if he is watched until he is eaten by his own Essence; Parasamgate.•

LIVING PRACTICE

Everything that we encounter is a demonstration of the Dharma; the demonstration of *Parikalpita* and *Paritantra* is constantly enacted. It is like watching crazy people watering a garden that is not there and getting angry if you step on the flowers. This is the garden of our everyday lives constructed from habit energy and exclusive identity and is why practice does not have to be relegated to isolation and private moments.

…out of relativity;
There was never a hare's horn so it neither exists nor does not exist; but the eternally unthinkable has a positive connotation:
    "*Why do all things cease to exist?*" [temporarily admitting objects]
    "*Because their not having self-substance (independently) makes it impossible to take hold of them*" [eliminating objects]
    If there is no seeing *Yathābhūtam*, conceptuality-as-reality enters.
    "*Why are all things impermanent? Because as soon as they take forms [or appear with individualized marks], they assume the nature of impermanence.*"
    They are co-operatively displaced moment to moment; here, integral with attention, memory which is always moving.
    "*Why are all things permanent? Because though they take form [or appear with individualized marks], they take [really] no such forms, and in reality there is nothing born, nothing passing away.*"
    They are permanent because there are no things as the Eternally Unthinkable which is the thingless Source; like father like son.
    So, all is differentiated and empty as such is the same as all is undifferentiated and full, which is unthinkable…any other position would be nihilism or eternalism; a negative object or a positive object.
    As *Yathābhūtam*, it is the Self Substance original Being eternally unthinkable mysterious thing. Tathatavastu, unborn, is positively asserted.•

YATHĀBHŪTAM

FANDANCE

Tath-agata – Thus come
Tatha-gata – Thus gone
Tathagata – One who has come from nowhere and goes nowhere

"The son of man has nowhere to lay his head."

Now-here
No-where
Nowhere

Gate, Gate, Paragate, Parasamgate…the smile; then the roaring laugh from the mountain peak of Malaya to the three periods of time. •

B.T.W. II

The Alayavijnana, Citta, Mind, is the ground where the idea of inside/outside is form-ed through the creative time-lock gesture. No-self is only in response to misplacement. Renunciation is paradoxically, to be your Self or you will only review your self as you were; acquiring your self; mistaking a thief for your own son. The gesture of the split in the Manovijnana brings forms; appearances, where causality prevails. It is an incessant split in time/no time. This is the builder of the house.

The overall gesture of compassion is not the alleviation of pain per se, but the alleviation of the gesture of pain; the misunderstanding that engenders the comical phantoms that surround themselves with *The World*. If pain is addressed conventionally, it will only produce dependence.

The Misjudgment

Self Realization is blocked in any school of Buddhism or Advaita that maintains that there is any thing outside the Mind.

Memory, for the unenlightened, is a narcotic. Succession becomes the reanimated corpse.

The Concomitance

"The world is unreal
only Brahman is real
the World is Brahman" –The Vedanta

"The wise do not see the erroneous world nor is there any reality in the midst of it. But since the erroneous world is reality, there is reality in the midst of it." – The Lanka

The only way that this paradox is resolved is in the absence of the *misplaced "you"*. We have to do something to make this world appear. That is Maya. Maya is not something in the world; an illusion produces no effects. All things are unborn because they are not things. All is impalpable; you can only attempt to prove anything only after you have asserted it and created the categories for its existence. The perceived cannot cognize or perceive. These are all of our discriminations. This seems to be easier to see when we set-up lab experiments where the observer is the indispensible link in the result but it is hard to see that our entire field of cognition is a set-up. Metaphysical irresponsibility is the biggest stumbling block to seeing Yāthabhūtam.

Unborn is not the opposite of born nor subject to the principle of causation.

Things removed from the three times are not born or unborn

Remember that the mark of insanity is seeing things; and it does not just apply to phantasmagoria. It is like debating existence or non-existence in the conjuring of a magician where your attention and perceptions have been carefully guided.

All of these negations are just to avoid the blind alleys and the dead ends. They all ultimately lead to a boundless affirmation/feeling, uncontained.

You open your eyes and without reference to anything that has ever happened, your hand reaches for the glass. The hand implies the glass and vice versa. This can only be an inside job; it cannot be matched any other way except in tortured imagination. The lynch pin of relativity and imagination is where we stand with the big red nose and floppy shoes.

Prajna

"The Bodhisattva who aims to be great in his spiritual disciplines is required to be perfect in the following four things:

1. He must have a penetrating comprehension as regards the nature of the manifestation of Mind.

2. He must be free of such notions as birth, abiding and destruction.

3. He must observe that external objects do not exist.

4. He must earnestly desire a state of realization by directly seeing into the inmost Self."

Compassion

"All things are, in their nature, from the first, unborn, unproduced, devoid of individualizing (indivi-dual-izing)* marks, have never been combined, are never dissolved, nor extinguished, nor changing, nor ceasing, and are lacking in self-substance…" …of themselves, of themselves!

Any-thing that is born has to come from somewhere, which can never be found; ever; the fault of non-finality.

* - My emphasis

Anutpattika-Dharma-Kshanti

Anything sought outside the concatenation is the product of discrimination; parikalpita only. There is only the unborn Reality.

Mutual dependence/interdependent origination is a bondage; *vasanas* of concatenation, habit energy/memory; an avoidance of Mind-only.

Things originate only after we put on the red nose and floppy shoes.

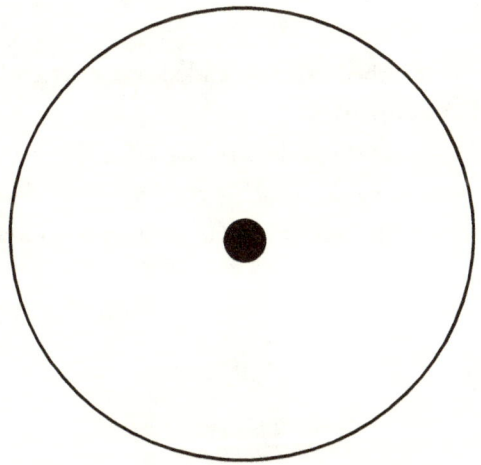

Self, Mind-only, is imagined as an individual self; a contracted exclusive perspective that never happened; a constantly maintained container with individual memory, accumulated and directed upon that supposition; thus an inhabited historical container all within and defined by its source,
It is no wonder that death is such a puzzle.
It is like fooling a child with a shell game where there is no pea.

Note: in the above drawing; if the center is removed, the circumference is unnecessary.

The Absolute Unthinkable becomes the subject when there is a collapse through the expression of apparent objectivity; this subject/object duality that must maintain its exclusive imaginary location.

The whole world is absorbed in Transcendence; the state of perfect bliss in which existence has its origin.

"If it's already manifest, what's the use of meditation? And if it is hidden one is just measuring darkness." – Saraha

But this is not obvious unless the doubter is doubted; the struggling center. •

BRAHMA/SHIVA

The world is always already dissolved; with the gaze of purusha there are as many ins as there are outs; nothing left hanging around.

Mind-blink: $\int L^3 dt = L^3 t \longrightarrow \partial/\partial t\, (L^3 t) \longrightarrow L^3$
$\phantom{\text{Mind-blink:}\quad}$ space $\quad$ time $\qquad\quad$ time $\qquad$ space

Chandogya Upanishad – gold ornaments
    Noumenon (gold) is not lost in the phenomenon (ornament) as are milk into curds. Fa Tsang's golden lion is a restatement of this. In fact, esoteric Buddhism like the Lankavatara is a restatement of Upanishadic philosophy in the idiom of the times, reflecting the perspective and emphasis that addressed the corruption and misunderstanding that comes with the incompetence of the "ignorant and simple minded". *Manas* in Buddhism is the *Antakarana;* a temporary formation between Spirit and matter imagined as independent existence. *Tathagathagarba, Alayavijnana* is *Brahman* veiled by *Manas/Antakarana,* which is the Granthi; the knot in the Heart; the misplacing of the Source. They were all steeped in Upanishadic philosophy and got away from it in name only since reform movements never retain the same terminology. Those who see Yatabhutham-Matra are not a fan (fanatic) of any tradition, exclusively, and will easily see this.
    There is no *practice* of Awareness, all is always already Awareness unshakable.* All "practices" lead to checking-up on results; "the thief dressing-up like a policeman to catch a thief". But the practice of no-practice through the inversion of attention is a serious quest; the separation of Consciousness as Consciousness for the origin and support of one's own Being. All is flashing on this Source, viewed either as estrangement or falling into the locus of manifestation** as the Source. Here individuality is not lost; just disowned; food and enjoyment of the Eternal Unthinkable.
    Birth; Manifestation of a temporary structure.
    Death; Un-manifestation of that structure; why not fear birth?
    The ego is a mediator making us think that we must have a separative relationship with what we cognize rather than a non-objective relationship.

* see Ho tse's jewel in *The King's Question*
** see the special seat of Consciousness in *The King's Question*

The joyous lake*; the Hridayam, is an intensifying crystal that magnifies its own omnipresence, the way the colors of light are revealed by a prism, and seems to interface at the sinoatrial node of the heart to the right of the breastbone. The feeling of Awareness here is intense enough to dissolve all things as they arise; being-on-time because of its coincidence with prebifurcated Awareness itself. Thoughts and feelings do not have to be approved or disapproved by a false or displaced center. *Brahman is the essence and secret of all existence.*** Brahman Hearts the universe; its beat keeps time through appearance/dissolution, motion. This is not an ego in the Skanda's or anything that can be viewed, placed or separated; so the esoteric traditions can stop arguing…a rose by any other name. *"Fools are taken in by the notion of giving a body to the Transcendental Being."*
– Tripura Rahasya

---

* Chandogya Upanishad
** We can change Brahman to any word we want.

MORE SPIRITUAL MATH

LYNCH PINS
Inversions, Imaginaries & Transcendentals

It's always amazing how an independent self-consistent system of thought; mathematics, can mirror the very process of manifestation and source through the revelation of functions and their inverses; the mathematical resolution of duality that always neutralizes itself to the ground of its own identity, i.e. Ln x; e^x - $\int$; d/dx – f(x); arc function – x^n; $\sqrt{x^n}$; etc.

Another interesting case is the seemingly harmless; x + 1 = 0, which is the hole in the ice that takes us outside the system itself; the isolated "x" being $\sqrt{-1}$, a doorway to another dimension where $\sqrt{-1} = i$ can be "brought back" through the squaring function; orthorotated back to the "real" system'; $i^2 = -1$. The clue is right here buried in this innocent expression (x + 1 = 0) until brought to its ultimate conclusion in an attempt to isolate "x", that nothing can give us $\sqrt{-1}$. Something inside the system always points to something outside the system as source point; something more fundamental. All of the mathematical resolutions of interdependent operations previously mentioned above make everything tentative and reducible to its ground; their interdependent reality has been pointed to. The most remarkable example of this is the transcendental function $y = e^x$ which becomes the still point equal to its own derivative and integral.

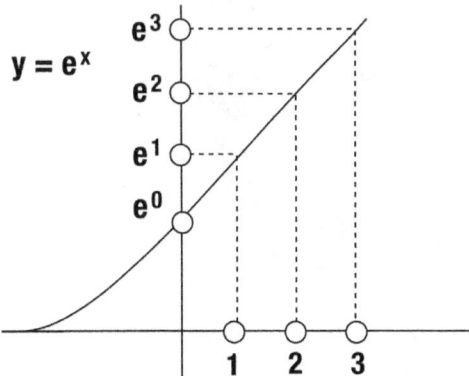

Anything but e (2.71828...) misses the coincidence; e^x, where e≠2.71828... misses the coincidence. Of course, the "x" in e^x does not have to be an integer.

YATHĀBHŪTAM

Just like there must be a base (2.71828...) to the transcendental function that is coincident with its integral and derivative; which is tantamount to saying that it is coincident with its source, the awareness of self at its locus point is coincident with its own origin and cannot be an object to itself and is now in a position (host) to be aware of and cancel all displaced centers which become objects to it. •

TEN

Haiku
This hard-shelled world can be penetrated without firing a shot.

Broadside
There is no separate one behind our words speaking or behind our eyes looking. What arises is not to any thing and this dizzy dance is much more intimate than it appears.

Bone
Now that you have witnessed the arising of all possibilities,
what is there left for you to be?

Transfiguration
What I am can never be seen;
an embarrassing position to be in;
a relentless embarrassment,
glowing into luminosity,
choking itself into transcendence,
rupturing into bliss.

Hiding Place
No way in or out of this wonder.
The great bliss swells
as the immensity;
its delight in everything imaginable and perceptible.
How long can we hold off from splitting into familiarity;
that cushion that crumbles eternity and makes us wonder
in our own dream.

Murmur
Deep in the secret cavity of the Heart, there is a moan of perfect pleasure and timeless fulfillment.
You thought that you were alone until it gives itself away.
It is from this audible murmur that everything is en-joyed.
You feel it; thoughtlessly, orgasmically thumping your Heart and brain with careless unsociable bliss; touching you like a friend in the dark.

Un-Found-Dead
How can an object,
any kind of object; physical, mental, apparitional,
be your Self? Who would be looking?
Destroy the "world" by leaving everything alone.

Presence
There is a truly hidden side to all of this; unnoticed and unsuspected. If we remain wide open, eternity will dissolve our granite life and make light of all the assembled silliness of tortured imagination.

Un-mis-take-able
Try to imagine a physical or mental object generating Awareness/presence; you automatically beg the question*; unmistakable.

*petitio principii

Vasana; The perfume
The mother of all addictions is being and non-being, birth and disappearance and creation and destruction. Every other kind of addiction is a further development of this. •

LANKA-YOGACARA

Absolute Idealism - Idealistic Realism
| |
Cittamatra   Vijnanámatra

Absolute Idealism leads to fearlessness; no-thing lying around to create the other; that moment when fear arises.

What swells then is the *Only*, unpinched to it full potential, throbbing and flashing in the house of its own creation.

The Lanka is a desperate plea through the haze of emotional and intellectual prejudice to insee the Eternal Unthinkable with minimal recourse to epistemology. •

ADVAITIC CHRISTIANITY

circle; Consciousness/Eternal Unthinkable

dotted line; apparent bifurcation that is infused with the nature of Consciousness itself that becomes Awareness resolved in its own manifestation moment to moment; the Father, the Son and the Holy Spirit.

The Father: Consciousness; the Purusha

The Son: Awareness as Creation; manifestation, Prakriti

Holy Spirit: The flavor of bliss that infuses everything with the mark of the Father; the Amrit; Chetana.•

ADVAITIC CHRISTIANITY 2

Resurrection Insurrection

"He who understands these sayings shall not taste death."

"You have dismissed the living ONE who is before you and you have spoken about the dead."

"The Kingdom of the Father is spread upon the earth and men do not see it."

"When you see Him who was not born of woman, prostrate yourselves upon your face and adore Him; He is your Father."

"Blessed is he who was before he came into being."

"When you make the two one…then shall you enter the Kingdom."

The kingdom is within you and it is without you. If you will know yourselves then you will be known and you will know that you are the sons of the Living Father." - Gospel of Thomas

…he shall not taste death…not because the Man is going to save you. We *are* the *Unborn;* there is no one to die.

This is the esoteric teaching; the exoteric teaching is that the one who uttered these words is the power and authority that reforms your bones or dust at the trumpet call; all because of their inability to understand the esoteric teaching. Worship the messenger and then kill him into immortality.

Sayings like these are a revelation of a present, perfect Condition, not the future promise of an exclusive authority.

Satan symbology:
The so-called great blasphemy is "wanting to be like God"; Satan/Lucifer. This is because God is conceived as an other. But God is perfect Presence; so it is like impersonating someone who is in the room and not noticing that he is there. There is no need to be "like" God which is standing outside of ME.

Satan/the Devil is the tendency to try to contain the Source and then vacillate between guilt-laden worship and megalomania.

ADVAITIC CHRISTIANITY 3

"Whoever finds the explanation of these words will not taste death."

"Let him who seeks, not cease seeking until he finds, and when he finds, he will be troubled, and when he has been troubled, he will marvel and he will reign over the all." - Gospel of Thomas; Log 14-18

...he will not taste death because he will have seen that he has never been born.

"You have dismissed the Living (ONE) who is before you and you have spoken about the dead." – G.O.T.

...Host; Living One, Guest; the dead.

"Whoever has known the world has found a corpse and whoever has found a corpse of him the world is not worthy." - G.O.T.

"By regarding the world as always like a magically moving corpse...one is emancipated". The Lankavatara Sutra, P-83

"The images are manifest to man and the light which is within them is hidden in the image of the light of the father. He will manifest himself and his image is concealed by his light."

...He will manifest himself; the world, and his image (the Source) is concealed by his manifestation.

The Father; The Mind-King •

MORE INVERSIONS

From red shift to paradigm shift

When phenomenal space is considered, the omnipresent gravitational distortions around the masses proposed by General Relativity could easily account for the red shift which would appear recessional only if a Euclidean paradigm were adopted. If this were done, the red shift could then be seen as dimensional rather than recessional; an expanding time vector of the present, timeless, creational matrix. The consequences of not understanding it this way would be the standard clueless linear progression from a magic singularity or uncaused object with infinite potential existing nowhere, since space itself emerges from it.

In objective space there always has to be a point of origin from where it is receding subject to the relativity of distance, time, length and their ultimate resolution at "C"; where objectivity dissolves. Dimensionality would render these difficulties moot. •

THE CONDITIONAL

The principal of the transverse spectator engenders cause and effect as paradigm, where there is something out of something, out there, that is never seen but since it is out there it must have happened when we were not looking; pre-quantum logic. From this the time periods are engendered to account for the unseen origin; everything becomes time conditioned.

    The principle of cause and effect where there is something out of nothing, an attempt to mollify the inexorable hall of mirrors which is non-finality, ultimately reduces to something out of something. Once the singularity appears without precedent we have the imagined time conditioned sciences. This is the conditional; an infinite regression or a magical appearance that begins its spacial and temporal processes through concatenation which is based on memory; immediate and recorded. •

THE UNCONDITIONAL

There is nothing outside of Mind; no world outside of Mind-itself. The Eternal Unthinkable is the ultimate longitudinal cause. Because it eliminates linear causation it is the *BE*-cause prior to the measurer, as potential plenum.

The Birth and Death of the Barren Woman's Child

The confusion about causation is that once we postulate "something", causation is a necessary and immediate by-product along with space/time whose raison d'etre is memory or recording as retrievable matrix embedded in the inevitable impression of passing time which allows for the Creation. This is how we deal with "something"; how we participate. But, what do we call something without where or when?

"*The highest Reality is an exalted state of Bliss.*" – Lanka, P-77

…the character of the Eternal Unthinkable.

Did you think that "you" would last as a set of attributes through all eternity? •

THE PIVOT

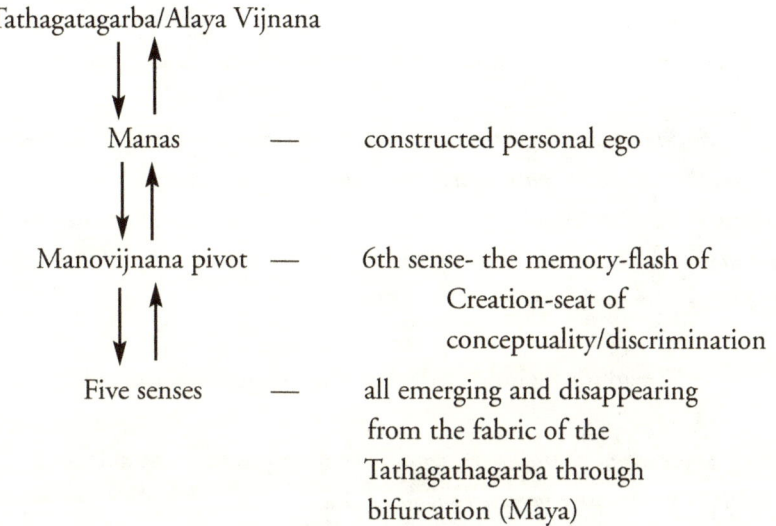

The Manovijnana is the recording/dividing mechanism that replaces the Alayavijnana with Manas after bifurcation. The in-formation from the senses which is the timeless appearance of Mind itself is housed and owned in the Manas which has no body of its own since all seeds are stored in the Alaya; Manas as temporary host.

The transcendence of the incessant parsing of the Manovijnana collapses the whole house of cards.

"I enter not into nirvana by means of being, work, of individual signs; I enter into Nirvana when the Vijnana which is caused by discrimination ceases." Lanka P-109. •

ETERNAL UNTHINKABLE

If objects are not things in themselves, how can Consciousness/Awareness be a thing-in-itself? When the cat finally catches its tail, it is all cat.

> *"My Mahayana is neither a vehicle, nor a sound, nor words; it is neither the truth, nor emancipation, nor the realm of imagelessness. Yet the Mahayana is a vehicle on which the Samadhi's are carried leading to various creative activities; the several forms of the will body are adorned with the flowers of the sovereign will."*

The Samadhi's are unlocked when the Granthi is dissolved.

> *"Those who, regarding the world as evolving from causes and conditions…fail to understand my teaching."* Lanka

…it is the moment-to-moment discrimination that is the causes and conditions.*

He who regards things external as transient is doomed to ruin. If this is avoided there is neither causation nor reality. Deliverance is where there is no objective world. •

---

*see the retroactive deception in *The King's Question*.

EX-SISTERE

All of the multiplicity of objects that are imagined are a function of memory and discrimination and regarded as existing outwardly until Consciousness/Awareness is fully engaged undistracted, without mediation. That objects are always as such, independently, is a myth; so things are not as they seem or otherwise.

"If [transcendental] knowledge fails to see, through various obstructions far and near, its own unique object that does not present itself [as an object], such is to be called wrong knowledge." Lanka P-148

"There is something that is not to be seen by the discrimination of its being, nor is it to be known as non existent; such is the Self-Essence of all things." Lanka P-164.

…the essence of all cognition; the functioning of Mind itself, is not in the condition of anything it perceives; if the essence of perception could be returned to light, darkness could not be perceived. The source of all cognition cannot be an object to itself and all objects of cognition and their source are not objects of any kind outside of conceptuality/concatenation. This is why in the *Len Yen Ching*, immediately after it was stated that objects "are not the perception" it was stated that "if objects are not the perception why do I see them?" This is the relentless caveat against making an object out of subject; the essence of perception. As Prajna, things are the cognizing of them; iteratively. Again, the mathematics of discrimination through the observation/discrimination operator: $\partial/\partial t\, L^3 t = L^3 = \int \partial/\partial t\, L^3 t = L^3 t$, the fundamental process (observation/memory) and the fundamental theorem. So as Prajna there are no things or objects of any kind; it is enlightened resolution. Everything that is imagined lying around is the past, which is the only accessible time. With *Parikalpita* and *Paritantra* the world does not fade out because mnemonic access is instantaneous and is socially agreed upon to be extant, and consequently, Source is virtually unnoticed… *"they do not recognize that their teaching is materialism because of their stupidity."* – Lanka P-151 •

THEATER

The bifurcated *Citta* is a dancer.
The *Manas* is her court jester.
and the *Manovijnana* and the five are the set designers.
This is the model for our theatrical preoccupation.
"The bodhisattva/Mahasattva does not regard name as reality and appearance as non reality"
Name is the time/space bound concept that is always late for Reality, and appearance or all forms of cognition are what is seen of *Mind* itself. •

350 PT. HALVETICA BOLD

The clueless cling to names, ideas and signs in Mind itself, feeding on multiplicities of objects; fueled and fooled by the notion of an exclusive ego-soul and what belongs to it. This clinging is evidenced by the inevitable Karma born of greed, anger and folly; a self-correcting system that responds to the imbalance and makes corrections from the ground of perfection. In a closed system, or no real place to go, there is transmigration fueled by this perspective; the motion of a water-bearing wheel unable to move forward. With the schism of ego and its belongings intact, all must seem to come from someplace; so I'svara, time, atoms or a supreme spirit. The clueless cannot even imagine that it comes from discrimination; the imagined prisoner in a flesh cage surrounded by a *World*.

> "The goose is out of the bottle." •

YATHĀBHŪTAM

SHEDDING LIGHT AND LOSING TIME

The photon is not 3-dimensional since all time/space (length)* cancels at "C", and all light is clocked at "C" regardless of whether you are approaching or departing from it.

If the photon (light) is not 3-dimensional, you are not measuring the speed of light but the limit of speed in 3-D; which is where you are measuring from. Something which does not have 3-D reference cannot have speed; s=vt, which is a 3-D concept.

If time is energy as well as mass is; $M=E/C^2$, it is because it is the gateway to source, the time realm being a symbol for the unknowable.

If it is the gateway to source, which coincides with the unknown present, serial time is its stepchild called by the same name; an adoption glorified and legitimized through mnemonic reference. Mass/Energy is 3-D which passes the threshold $h/4\pi$; time/light is not. •

---

*see Quantum Vindications in *The King's Question*.

THE FREQUENCY/TIME AMBIGUITY

A frequency, whose vibratory rate is faster, lets say, for a group of sentient beings, would possess the same "time sense" relative to their frame of reference* as perception, recording and playback. But, depending upon the frequency disparity, it could seem like the slower vibration frequency realm is standing still or frozen in time with no connection to "moving" events. This would reveal how much events are participatory in each frequency domain, i.e. who's moving them. So for the higher frequency the lower frequency would have no time line and because of their dimensional advantage could manipulate the lower frequency's "past" and "future". Moreover, since the lower frequency could not see the higher frequency, it would be attributed to "other" causes.

These frequencies, of course, would not be frequency variations within the same realm like variations in Hertzian radio frequencies, but in total higher space/time continuum vibrations.

So "time travel" is the perspective of different relative frequencies off the isolated linear time-line with the advantage going to the higher frequency. Seeing "all time at once" is the relative perspective of a higher frequency or "Higher Self".

Whether this "higher" perspective is a natural habitat or an acquired skill, it is obvious how the mysterious "gravity" is connected to the latter; the flame frozen in a gravitational field, the "still".

Whatever gravity "is", when we move "with" it we are embraced without stresses. This might be a clue to its pedigree.

With the advent of Quantum Mechanics and Bell's theorem, the skeleton is no longer in the closet; the conventional physicist and the fundamental religious practitioner of all religions are. The skeleton is walking about. •

---

*see Quantum Vindications in *The King's Question*.

YATHĀBHŪTAM

BISHOP BERKELEY

"Esse Est Percipi"

"To be is to be perceived."

    This is the great misunderstanding of the ultimate import of *esse est percipi* and radical idealism in general. This is certainly not solipsism and it is not the facile implication of "to be is to be perceived" because this makes things and their observation, two things. To pose a question like "does a falling tree in the forest make a noise if there is no one there to hear it" is to already reduce it to the terms of materialism and assume that this presumption is already proven, using it as an axiom to frame the question. *Petitio Principii*. This certainly would not be allowed in Q.M.; even in the conservative interpretation. The true question would be "does a falling tree in the forest make a noise if there is no one there to *here* it"?; the sound question is secondary to the manufacturing of a permanent independent place-in-space that can be imagined to exist outside of present Awareness. We can imagine the lives of the characters in a "holideck" program going on after the program is shut down. We can view a visual recording of what we did as file memory in real time, or the impalpable present as no time.

    But wait, you say; are you telling me that there is no *forest* by itself, right now? Welcome to the 21st century and the abandonment of the manipulation and substitution of concepts for Reality.

    "The electron is not a wave with material properties; it is a wave of probability. We can also call it a particle, but its position and momentum (mass x velocity) cannot be known simultaneously". [$\Delta x \cdot \Delta p \geq h$] because h is a constant.

    So we either do not know where it is but something is moving; or we have an idea where it is and it is not moving; which is of course impossible; impossible only if we are talking about independent things. And finally: "the electron is a wave; exhibits the properties thereof, when we are not looking, and a particle; shows location, when we are looking." Do we still believe that this is happening outside of Mind?

All is manufactured; made, concocted; goods, services, reality itself as we know it; manufacturing consent through all the constructs we have been examining. *Fatto a Mano; Fatto a Conscio.* But we have forgotten the Source and slipped into an image-anary center. The common man exists beside himself. •

INTRODUCTION TO THE SUMMATIONS

One would be hard-pressed to find anything closer to the true Dharma eye than the Buddhism of the Lankavatara, the Hinduism of the Tripura Rahasya and the Ati-Yoga texts of Dzogchen. The Lanka is almost free of metaphor as is the most important parts of the above-mentioned sources; straight talk that must be received into the resonation of the source.

The repetitions are extremely important. •

Σ
THE MIND IS MOVING

A free rendering of the spirit of the Lankavatara

Holding on to the Cobra

The root of delusion is nourished by memory which is the seat of the objective cage that produces the fool. The original Source is beyond anything imaginable; the Mind-King. With the Paravritti or turning around, one is in the Lotus of the Heart of Reality.

Without discrimination, nothing moves; there are neither things nor no-things; there is the absence of no-thing which swallows up the false subject. A personal soul cannot stand apart from its subject or source which reduces it to a phantom or reflection. All is not within all; everything that we cognize is not within itself! There is nothing here but thought construction; nothing has ever been in existence; *ex-sistere*. It is the unborn; the barren woman's child.

Nothing has been born; nothing will be born and no causation to mediate; one Self-Nature removed from speculation and thought construction; the fireflies of the enchanted

Nothing has ever originated in causation; it is only from the gesture of bifurcation that all multiplicities appear and have to be accounted for if lulled into the sleep of discrimination and the non-acceptance of the relative reality of space/time.

There is [One Thing] that produces and is above all multiplicity; an essence hidden inside, in a manor of speaking, all that have body. It is in the intermingling of causes and conditions that the stupid imagine the birth of all things but these causes and conditions have no causes and conditions. It is the addiction to discrimination where the field of mentation gets confused and it is imagined that there is something to take hold of without ever questioning the holder; the "cheese that stands alone". The holder always gets a free pass; this is the arrogance of stupidity. When the Mind is released from conditions and thought of separate self, it no longer arises as a reflex in the body and the world goes with it; like the voice from a radio, there is neither an ego, a being or a person inside.

The entire universe or triple world (desire, form and formlessness); the embodiment of the compassion of sense forms, the manifested visual forms and the unborn emptiness of the Pure Perfect Presence, has nowhere to place itself within or without; it is homeless.

It is the manifestation of potential and its unmanifestation. Suchness does not distinguish the discriminated from the discriminating or all so-called things have no self-existence. Nothing whatsoever is born or ceases to exist by reason of causation. Looking for a cause for something that already exists is pointless and is a symptom of the moving Mind; as memory, space/time, concatenation and thought construction.

Causation: like a five minute delay on a musical effects box, the one sound is at two times; inseparable. This is how there is karma without causation; *chi la fa, l'aspetto.* We do not see that it is always already done; *he who does it, waits for it.* Because of sequential perception/memory, we create/imagine a past in which it was caused upon our rehearing, even though it is a re-presentation. Linear causation is a product of a perceived gap of accountability modeled on our mode of perception; it was a non-event before its projection and collapse into time.

The Substance and its Function is separated and externalized. It is not that one should keep off the idea of birth and disappearance which *take place* in causation; but one is to keep away from the wrong imagination as to causation itself. It is because "things" or isolated blocks of recorded perception are linked by suggested iterative concatenation (causation) that this is imagined. But no establishment is needed; it is the absence of no-thing (try to imagine that!)

There is no self-nature, no thought construction, no reality, no Alaya Vijnana. These are for spectators who are not admitted to the Mahayana. Vasana or memory are the waves of Mind producing the forms.

An individual mind is evolved by clinging to the appearance of Mind itself where the visible world cannot be outside this source. This clinging is the reflection of *Manas;* but the gate to the highest reality has nothing to do with subject/object.

"Discriminating discrimination" is looking into discrimination itself where minds are saturated with the forms of ignorance. Looking into the nature of discrimination takes no prisoners; the personal soul, continuity, the skandas, causation, atoms, the supreme spirit, the ruler, the creator; all go.

Mind is all; all that these discriminations serve to do is to usurp the Mind-King. Things are not as they seem, nor are they otherwise. If they were otherwise, *they* would be something else. Giving names to appearances will make them last forever. Delusion never occurred but we immediately go to sleep when appearances are marked and stored. All these individual objects have never been born but they are not non-existent. The mind of sentient beings will perceive something like objective reality and most will be fooled. When we open up to transformations we know where all this is.

Through perception and form the imaginative "self substance" is declared, and standing alone needs to origin-ate; now all is distorted; self and world; the barrier between that which perceives and that which is perceived; again demanding origination. The mind is agitated by memory, and not knowing what it is, time/space become real.

Suchness is all there ever was. The Mahayana is not definite but set in motion by the thoughts of beings. All things are always unattainable and resolved in their cognition, discrimination to discrimination.

CAUSALITY REQUIRES SOMETHING TO ALREADY EXIST AS A CAUSAL AGENT AND THEREBY POSTULATES SOMETHING UNCAUSED AND DESTROYS ITSELF.

Even to discriminate purity is to be established in egotism. For the hearers, there is the teaching of transitoriness but this is only the spoken teaching. One hand is still holding on and the Mahayana is still untangled. When memory is misunderstood and is king, there rises something taken for real existence and the birth of realities. It is the discrimination of external objects possessing* individual marks independent of the perceiver. It is not birth that is the issue here, but perception and the inevitable enquiry as to who is perceiving. Is the perceiver different or the same as what is perceived? If it is the same, there is no perceiver. If it is different, there is no perception; the barrier to the "object" would be total.** But all things are the cognizing of them without a cognizable per

---

* see Fruitful Negations in *The King's Question*
** see Full Circle in *The King's Question*

ceiver; (which is only a time conditioned conceptual afterthought) and therefore anything perceived. This, of course, is always the case outside of time and space; what is intuited as the present and is the functioning of the Mind-King.

The process of bifurcation allows us to taste the presence that cannot be cognized; the King and his subjects who are perceived as objects. Maya, Citta, Intelligence, tranquility, the dualism of being and non-being...for whom are these teachings and of what significance? This the Buddha's deafening roar; and the Mahayana as such, disappears. The inner realization; the will body, has no mnemonic reference, as the primary. The triple world and nirvana are in this body and all is the realm of Mind; when all is understood error neither arises nor ceases. The error, or the world, is discriminated; none of it stands on its own. When these forms and figures are all yours, they are purified. Causation is not a law as such; it is something to be under-stood and transcended. The error of misunderstanding memory produces the notion of externally existing objects and the Mind-King is obscured. In error, mind is produced from Mind. Thinking delusion is separate from truth is the disease of the mind. Truth is where Maya is observed in its proper bearings; the "object", Samskrita, is seen devoid of qualified and qualifying, unpredicted; the asylum of suchness where all the realms are reviewed with Prajna. Emptiness is not a condition or anything that can be imagined; it is a warning sign.

Knowledge is the abandonment not the destruction of the discriminated; it was never there to be destroyed. Nothing is born and yet things are being born; they are born as abstractions; concepts of name focused on the appearance of Mind as memory. In Yathābhūtham there is full participation prior to abstraction where all apparent things are set free and empowered; then they die or are de-formed and left with a name, like a body that disappears leaving just the clothes; the mystery is complete. Do not ask where something went, ask if it was ever there. Self-discrimination sets all false reasonings in motion through iterative recording of what we see, hear, think and understand. But the existent cannot be qualified with being and non-being. When what is imag-ined is further developed, causal origination arises as a doctrine of accountability. Suchness is no other than discrimination and discrimination is no other than appear ance when parikalpita and paritantra are disengaged. Memory is the seed of recognition; re-cognition, re-experiencing the recording of the discrimination of an imagined outer world. Things are just a combination of self-seed and the imagination of an external world. We can *see* the mythology being created everywhere; any time we look. The abandonment of ego-attachment is recognition not an event. When there is no one to die…"*he shall not taste death*".* The Alayavijnana and the Vijnana system; there is something externally appearing; this inner support, but it was never external; neither being nor non-being so not even momentariness (of what!). No thought construction, no substances—nothing obtains in Mind-only. The uncertainty of the quantum world is that they can no longer be considered "things"; the laws of visible things do not apply; they are only potentials which are not so obvious in the macro world and the centuries of the materialist perspective that everything was framed in. It was the microcosm that brought out the flaw. If there is not a single independent atom, unmeasured, in existence, there is no external world; the Von Neumann perspective closest to absolute idealism. We cannot get away from Mind in the same way that we cannot see our own eyes or bite our own teeth. No conscious effort can bring it about; no vehicle or one who rides it. All that sets the triple world in motion is Mind.

    The Mano-Vijnana and the five senses cut the "world" into pieces like a mad swordsman. Causation and the fourfold proposition have blinded the bewildered to Mind-only. Memory and concatenation is the quilt we wrap ourselves and is the origin of all things imagined; but the imagination itself has no reality so it does not really take place; it just takes place in memory like the fetching of fruit from the air. The Being realized by the wise has never been in existence and is not united with causation until things are asserted and become one with causation through memory and concatenation which is its dynamic. This puts the "perverted view of causation" to rest which has confused the philosophers since time immemorial by trying to imagine it as objective serial translation.

    Apparent objective reality is *Mind*, manifest; this is not imagination. The imagination is that it is out there and running on its own. The imagination is that the small mind has ever taken its rise. All things are causeless and unborn; are timeless and placeless. Time, space and causa-

* The Gospel of Thomas

tion are price tags. When things are seen as neither subject to causation nor above it*, then erroneous views are abandoned. Causality is only related to a system of mentality. Again, once something is asserted, the price tag is its origin which leads right to a perpetual regression; otherwise that thing depended upon would be causeless.** Check mate.

IF ALL OF THIS IS MIND, WHERE DOES THE WORLD STAND! With the turning back (paravritti) there is no dependence on anything. Not being born, suchness, reality, limit, emptiness; these are other names for form and there are none without bifurcation. Emptiness is no other than form; no birth is no other than birth which is complete revelation when the divider is absent. All of this implies not having any abode or place. When the small mind is not born all views are nonexistent. The elements of appearance are always the Mind.

"Discrimination of discrimination" is to make concepts of what has been separated which leads away from Nirvana. The small mind is a reflected image constructed from memory and is born of reality but not reality as it is in itself. It is the sravakas; the hearers, who are attached to the doctrine of causation. The "world" evolves from the separation of Mind and what belongs to it so the world appears to be *ELEMENT MADE INSTEAD OF MIND MADE.* Causation is the doctrine of the discriminators and is attachment to multiplicity as "ding an sich". But Reality cannot be embraced by any theory. If a cause must be asserted, it is the unborn/seeming born. When even momentariness is denied, it is just another swipe at conceptual categorical thinking; at the taking of the position of Dharma spectator. When all the senses are denied (Heart Sutra); it is to remove them as objective causes; rays from subject to object which is actually object to object, trying to bridge the gap between seer and seen.

The statement that blatantly proclaims the non-difference between the insights of the great Vedantic and Buddhist sages is stated in the Sagathakam #746: "*The Ego [atman] characterized with purity is the state of Self Realization; this is the Tathagata's womb (Garba) which does not belong to the realm of the theorizers*".

The centuries of bickering and petty squabbles is nothing but terminological mystification and low minded sectarian posturing. Here we

* if they were above it, they would still be things
** this is the essence of the Madhyamika

see Atma and Garba in the same sentence centuries before both religions were "developed". But an ego-soul is the final parsing of mistaken identity; the same gesture that divides the seer from the seen even though the gesture itself is a barren woman's child. The Skandas are discriminated in parikalpita and cannot be the container of an objective ego which amounts to a phantom within a phantom. All of this is objectivity/materialism; the seeking and attempted finding of the Source.

>Sagathakam #765:
>
>*"Those who hold the theory of non-ego (anatman) are the injurers of the Buddhist doctrines, they are given up to the dualistic views of being and non-being; they are to be ejected by the convocation of the Bhikshus and are never to be spoken to."*

The subtleties of Buddhism are in full force here, stepping right on a cherished distinguishing position; holding that the theory of no-self without full active understanding is worse than holding the theory of an ego in the Skandas. The closest linguistic indication or pointing finger that can be presented is the "absence of non-ego", where a double absence makes it impossible to conceptualize and for "you" to walk away.

>Sagathakam #768:
>
>*"Trying to seek in five ways for an ego-soul in the accumulation of the Skandas, the unintelligent fail to see it, but the wise seeing it are liberated."*
>
>...you see what you are not, and then the sought is the seeker.

The only cause is Mind; functioning. The objective world is not the cause of bondage. The created and the conditions of causality are unborn, not existing in the bifurcated field of perception. Unrealities cannot be causal agents. If the ego is perceivable, who would be the perceiver? Transformation is the actual state of ex-istence that is removed from birth and destruction.

>Sagathakam #847:
>
>*"One should first examine into the nature of an ego-soul and keep oneself away from attachment; to try to go beyond without an examination is of no more worth than a barren woman's child."*

Vedantic style Vichara is advocated as the practice of examination or enquiry.

Sagathakam #852:
"The Vijnana not being born there is no ignorance; ignorance being absent there is no vijnana, and how can succession take place?...it takes place in memory as Vasana.

The only evil one is delusion; Prapanca, which is the tendency to contain the source. All propositions, trivially reasoned, vacillate between guilt-laden worship and megalomania; small mind until suchness pertains and Mind-only is established.

The spirit of the advaitic perspective should never be trivialized and reduced to nihilism…no speaker or speaking or emptiness, no rising of the causation chain, no sense organs, Dhatus, Skandas, greed, objects; no deliverance, bondage; no time, Nirvana, Dharma Essence, no Buddhas, truths, fruition; no birth or passing away. By maintaining the Mind-only the *idea* of reality is removed. In Mind-only one escapes from being attached to emancipation. It does not reveal itself because of memory; *vasana,* where the error (the world) is substituted.

The elements are devoid of selfhood, ding an sich. An object does not make an object. From the very first, the Buddhas, Sravakas, and Buddha Sons have never been born; no past, present or future; a world without time.

A Buddha is not one born of the womb. This is the true virgin birth in all of the esoteric traditions. When the Mahayana is untangled the goose is out. •

Σ
ALL IS BRAHMAN/SELF

A free rendering of the spirit of the Tripura Rahasya

The Mystery

Realization of Self requires no concentration of mind; that is why the Self is not objectively knowable. Ignorance is the feeling of differentiation of the creator and created; which are only the details of the same Reality. Unending Awareness which is perpetually existing is your Self.

The Infinite and Unbroken contracts with the gesture of objectification. All is within; the container cannot be split-up by the contained. All appearance is insentient no matter what it is and cannot exist without pure Transcendental Self Shining Being whose Intelligent Bliss comes to the fore when the restless mind's dynamism is subdued.

The absence of Consciousness/Awareness cannot be conceived at any time since the proclamation of not being Aware requires Awareness. This abstract Intelligence is wider than space itself and is beyond subtle. Its nature is to glow as she displays the universe like images in a mirror. All that is manifest is not concrete since they have never been created. This unbroken 1-1 consciousness is Will *(Die Welt als Wille und Vorstellung)*, self-sufficient and independent which becomes Maya during Creation; which is not one "thing" changing into another but manifestation of Will/Idea. The images are in the mirror but the mirror is untouched by them.

Denial of the world is denial of the intelligence of the Source. There is no bondage, no liberation, no aspirant, and no process of attainment which always requires separation and judgment. No transient mental concept of devotion can produce intransient results of the highest truth. Investigation is the first step to indescribable Bliss; the Devi Tripura, the conscious core of the Heart, knows everyone intimately.

The bodiless Creator of the universe creates it without any external aid; and similarly when we investigate the Self remember who the investigator is; remembering that what is seen is absolutely nothing but sight and the significance of the Source being knowable and unknowable at the same time. Immortality is the right relationship between the knowable and the unknowable.

YATHĀBHŪTAM

Σ
THE CORE OF THE LENG YEN CHING*

A free rendering
The Absolute One Reality Eternal Mind reduces; bifurcation, thought.

The permanent and impermanent (appearance re-established moment to moment because of continuous reduction) unite to transform Mind into Alayavijnana or Store Consciousness with its three characteristics; (1) self-evidencing (basic ignorance), (2) the changing field of perception/cognition which is the parsing of fundamental wisdom into an imagined objective world of form which is the third. The world is the *face* of emptiness. When this false perception confronted form, a small portion of this form was gradually grasped as being self-possessed; a living "being"; so Mind seemed to be contained in form. Thus the cycle of births and deaths through the engine of basic ignorance.

Wrong use of a clinging mind and attachment to causal conditions screened the essence of Consciousness. Cognizance of all causal conditions as having no nature of their own is the state of true Mind. It is the false recognition of inner disturbance by stirring accumulated causes that is mistaken for the nature of Self-Mind; the mistaking of a thief for your own son.

All states that can be returned to imagined external causes are obviously not YOU. But what is "that" that cannot be returned anywhere? Each thing seen is an object but not the seeing; we cannot *see* our seeing. That seeing which is independent of objects is the essence of Consciousness and cannot be returned to any of its conditions; if it could this would render any or all conditions baseless and invisible.

When we see light our seeing is not clear. When we see darkness our seeing is not obscure. But even when our absolute seeing insees this relationship; this essence of seeing independent of objects, there is still a tendency *to perceive* this essence of perception as an independent object forgetting that all objects, as such, are not. •

* The Surangama Sutra in sanskrit.

DZOGCHEN

The All Creating King; The Dimension of the Pure Perfect Presence

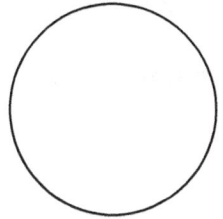

Causeless Thigle

Three realms:
Desire – of apparent body-embodiment of compassion of sense-forms
Forms –semi-apparent voice-visual realm (miracles)
Formlessness –Mind of ME-Pure Perfect Presence-Unborn Emptiness

Dharmakaya-abides without movement
Sambhogakaya-clarity beyond concepts
Nirmanakaya-transforms Presence everywhere

Dzogchen: *"Everything is an appearance which manifests from Pure Perfect Presence. Nothing other than that exists."*
Lankavatara: *"The world is what is seen of Mind itself."*

Pure Perfect Presence = Mind itself
The all creating Presence = Mind itself = ME; Presence and its qualities in perfection
Nothing to be renounced
No purification
No approach or achievement
No acceptance, rejection, struggle, achievement
Nothing is other than our own Presence; P.P.P.
The conception of attachment and the method of non-attachment are both recoil

You cannot be one with Pure Perfect Presence; you are Pure Perfect Presence.

"All phenomenon are already created in total effortless primordial liberation, the essence of ME, the all Creator."

Nothing develops as a serial spectacle;* it is only dissected after the fact and reorganized; the Mind is moving, not the wind or the flag.

* *"What's the point of looking for a cause for something that already exists?"* - Chandrakirti

The Yeshe Marmel Gyü

"Hey lord of secrets! Self-Perfection abides as the mass of your own Rigpa in the center of your Heart…"

…remember that the "House of Brahman" is the lotus of the Heart in the Upanishads.

The Sangye Dorje Sempa Tsigsumpai Gyü

"The clear Essence of one's Awareness is Samantabhadri Buddha – pure Emptiness beyond substance and color. The vividly present Essence of one's Awareness is Samantabhadri Buddha – clear, vivid, unceasing Awareness beyond nihilistic nothingness. One's Rigpa is Dharmakaya Buddha-abiding as the inseparability of vivid Awareness and empty Essence beyond substance. Because exactly one's vivid Awareness is Enlightenment, one should not search for some other enlightenment. Because one's vivid RIGPA is continuously radiant there is no action to achieve Dharmakaya Enlightenment."

… *"In this one word Awareness is the key to all mysteries."*
– Shen Hui (Ho Tse) – the "7th" Patriarch. •

RUMOR

Of all the mythologies what we embrace to account for the way that we think things are, the greatest one is "us"; wide circles constructed with one foot nailed to the floor. •

FINAL THOUGHTS

"To attend your own funeral" is to *see* what you thought you were.

••

If anything originates from that which has no origin, it is not anything. Memory is the sky-flower.

••

"When one analyses, there is nothing" – The Kunded Gyalpo

"Whenever the Mind functions you are spacializing the absolute" – Atmananda

••

Mind never departs from its transcendence; so all that appears to be never departs from its transcendence.

••

Since perceiv-ing and know-ing is what I am,
I can never be found, as such.
How do you improve upon perfection?
Everything adjusts to right understanding or delusion. •

ABOUT THE AUTHOR:

Born in Brooklyn, New York, Robert J. LaSardo (Sho-Fu) has combined a lifetime of scholarly and practial Buddhist devotion with his scientific and mathematical passions in this metaphysical study. An unusual combination of talents and focus, Sho-Fu has been able to find the connections between groundbreaking new science and the ancient wisdom of Buddhism and Vedanta.

Sho-Fu became a student and practicioner of Buddhism in 1966. He studied Zen in New York City with the legendary Yasutani Hakuun Roshi, the Dharma Heir to both Soto and Rinzai Zen schools (author of "Eight Beliefs in Buddhism"), as well as Soen Roshi and Eido Roshi, who gave him the name Sho-Fu ("Pine Breeze") in 1971 as an acknowledgement of his devotion to Buddhist practice.

He was fortunate to study Tibetan Buddhism with Geshe Wangal and was an original member of the Center of Oriental Studies in New York, where a variety of disciplines were taught by visiting Tibetan and Mongolian monks.

Sho-Fu began to study Taoist disciplines and philosophy with Mantak Chia in the 1980s and became a friend to the Ramana Maharshi Ashram through his relationship to the Ashram's teacher, Bhagwat (Arunachala Bhakta Bhagwat). In addition to a lifetime of meditation practice, including numerous Shessin, he has gone on retreat with Sheng-Yen, the Ch'an Master located in Queens, New York.

"Yathābhūtam" is the last part of the trilogy which includes "The Mind Seal, A Critical Examination of the Verses of the Lankavatara Sutra" (2008) and "The King's Question" (2010). All of Sho-Fu's books may be purchased on Amazon.com. •

www.ingramcontent.com/pod-product-compliance
Lightning Source LLC
Chambersburg PA
CBHW031656040426
42453CB00006B/320